THE DOORS WILL OPEN
By: Alastor Velazquez

THE DOORS WILL OPEN

First edition. December 16, 2024.

ISBN: 979-8230958468

Written by Alastor Velazquez.

I WONDER WHY
Hold me like a friend
Kiss me like a lover
I see the anguish in your eyes
The gray creeps in around the edges
It seeps into your soul
And you sway like a branch
Deep in the grove
And I stand there
With a stake in my hand
Held to my heart
I can't escape it
Pierce me with blue eyes
You see more in me
You see a warm spring
I cannot handle the weight
I cannot handle this weight
You tell me to lift it
You tell me to relieve it
You give me a shoulder
Tell me to cry
My body tries
My mind refuses
It's a steel trap
And I don't want to fall into it
A stray dog
Stuck in a vice
You hear the screams I don't let out
I wonder how
I wonder how
You tell me to cry
A few tears manage to slip out

I wonder why
I wonder why

LAY ME TO WASTE

Lay me to waste
I feel that sour distaste
Lay me to waste

Lay me to waste
Fuck
I hate this bitter taste
I feel like a waste
Like I want to leave
Without a trace
Lay me to waste
Fuck
Lay me to waste

GOD, DO YOU LOVE ME?
God, do you love me?
I whisper in my mind
I see his back

Cause I feel like I'm falling behind
Do you know my daddy slapped my behind?
And you remind me of love
So god above
Do you love me?
Do you hear me when I weep?
Did you see me?
When I had to creep up stairs?
Did you see?
When my daddy was being a creep?
Do you know how bad
I wanted to run into the street?
Did you look at me in the shower?
Did you watch as I cowered?
Do you see me as a coward?
And did you see me dancing?
With no clothes on at 6 years old
Did you look at my chest when I got cold?
How was I to know?
How was I to know?
And
Did you actually watch me grow?
Do you see me in the mirror?
Did you know I was supposed to fear her?
Did you see what I had to bear?
Did you see what I had to bare?
Do you even care?
God
Do you love me?
The way that I love the trees
The way I love the dead grass
Beneath my feet

The way I love the flowers
And will you too tower over me?
Or are you small like me?
Do you really look like me?
God, do you love me?
And did you see me nude?
Do you think I'm rude?
Do you find dogs duct taped crude?
Do you find my daddy cruel?
I want to love you
Do you want to love me too?

NOT DEAD YET!
To you
In the mirror
I'm not dead yet

Don't give up on me
I'm not done yet
Hear me out
I'm still going
Please don't count me out
I don't want a body bag

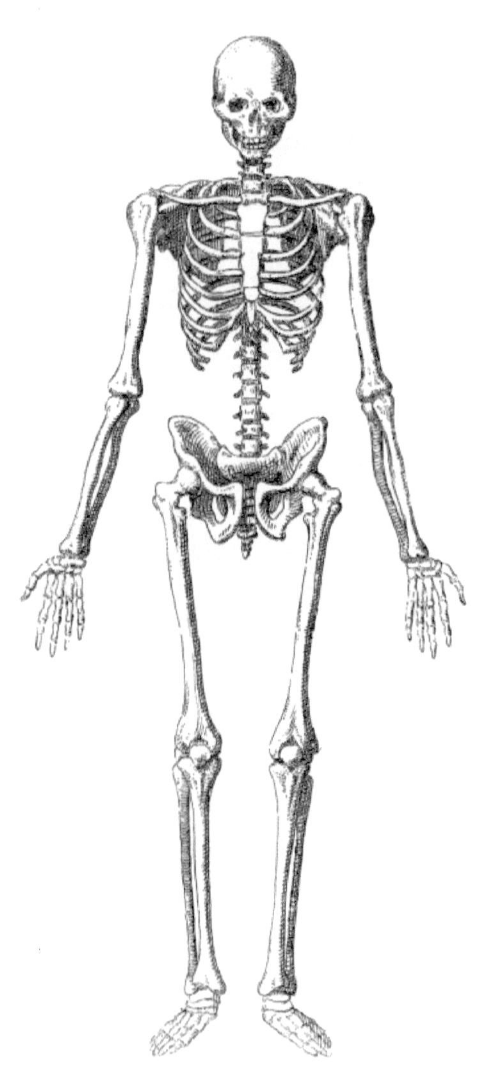

THE ANGLER
>The fish squirms and fights
>Against the line
>For food

For life
Desperate
Paramount
It's dragged against the current
Breaching the surface
He holds it up
5 pounds of bones
Flesh
He grins with stained teeth
Tossing it into the cooler
All that fight just to fail
Just to bathe in ice
And die

SHOULD I, SHOULD I
If I kill myself tonight
Would it be worth it
I truly think I might

Embrace me
Before I sink to the bottom
But what's lower than this?
I know what is
I've been down there before
Could I do it?
Would I do it?
If I never escaped
Would I still let you kiss my scars?
Would I still feel enough?
Would I still be enough?
Should I kill myself tonight?
Keep me from holding this knife to my throat
Should I cry myself to sleep tonight?
Expecting someone to cradle me
Knowing that they won't
Should I kill myself another time?
Do I deserve to make it to 25?
Go out and buy a gun
And I'll pull the trigger
My brains will splatter
Will it be enough?
Held against my teeth
And my jaw aches
Blank eyes staring into an iron sight
Can it be enough?
Can it bring me past the brink?
Breach the surface
Have your hand on the barrel
Maybe holding my fragile life
Between murderous fingers
Will make me feel alive

So it's not just me and a bullet
So I'm not alone
Will you kiss my broken
Bloodied lips
As you lay me down
Can my head rest on your chest
So the last thing I hear is a beating heart
And I'll play my death song
As I lay in my bed
A storm raging in my head
Thinking
Should I kill myself tonight

DANCING BLIND
I'm dancing in the dark
Terrified of falling apart
Do you see me?

Wanting to be free
Locked in a cage
Young man
Filled with rage
Will you still love me?
When I age
And will you still
Find me so strange
Or do you see all my pain
As I pace the streets
Because I love the rain
Do you see me?
Terrified to walk
Stuck in cement
Afraid to crawl
To go past that wall
Refusing to answer phone calls
I'm scared
I'm scared

WHY DO YOU HAUNT ME?
Who are you?
Tell me
Why do you trail after me
Why do you haunt my mind
Why do I not know your true name
Why do I barely know your face
Tell me
Phantom
Spirited one
What are you
Why do you wish to provoke me so
Why must I suffer
Tell me
Tell me
Why do you haunt me?

I DIVE IN
I dive into the river styx
Nick me with your love
Send me to cloud nine above

Prick me
Like I need you like medicine
I begin again
I begin again
With you
With you
Hex me with your gaze
Graze my side
Linger next to my bedside
Leave me blind
So that I dive in
I dive in
Like i'm diving in
To river styx
And you nick me
Trick me
Prick me
With your ketamine
Be my dopamine
Like I need you like medicine
I begin again
Keep my loneliness from happening
And I dive into styx
I dive in
Tear me apart
Tear me apart

RECTIFY
There's a dark cloud hanging overhead
Even with all these fucking meds
That I take
And I know I was overheard yelling and slamming doors
I feel like it lasted for hours
But it was mere moments
Do you see the dark clouds overhead
Hanging low and heavy
My cheeks streaked with tears
My face stricken with all my fears
Even as the rage boils over
And you have to take cover
I'm sorry you have to take cover
Rectify me
Exemplify me
Crucify me
Hold me accountable

I'M BOUND

Hold me accountable
Show me my insecurities
You know I'm not blind to them

You know I bind to them
I'm bound
Held down
And you see me drown
In the overhanging clouds
You see me drowning
In the overhanging clouds
You tell me you're proud
But all I see is the tree shrouding
You out
See that tall tree
Shrouding you out
There's a dark cloud hanging overhead
And it's so fucking heavy

YELLOW BIRD
Sing to me yellow bird
Oh won't you sing to me
I promise you are heard

And I know your song hurts
I know your throat burns
Yellow bird
Yellow bird
Sing sweet to me
Sing sweet to me
I promise to sit right here
To sit right here
To wipe away all your tears
Help conquer all of your fears
And I know it will take some years
But sing to me yellow bird
Let me hear your mellow words
I'll make sure your story's heard
Yell out to me
Spell it out to me
Won't you
Won't you
Sing to me yellow bird
I'll follow you
Yellow bird
Yellow bird
Sing for me

UNABLE TO FLY
It's okay not to cry
Don't be embarrassed
At your inability to fly
As long as you're not afraid
To still try
Sit still
Sit still
Give me your hand
I'll take the kill
I'll take the kill
It's okay not to fly
As long as you still try
As long as you still try
Forget the kill
Forget the kill
Give me your hands
Dear
Give me your hands
Slow
Flower petals
Fall
slow

GUNPOWDER LINED GUMS
gunpowder lined gums
Angels with sweet sour hymns
I cannot recall
I cannot recall
Just don't let go of my hand
Don't let me fall
Into these
Gunpowder lined gums
Let me sway
Let me stay
Let me just say
Angels scream in my ears
So loud that I cannot hear
Their white gaze burns me
It burns me
Charcoal my skin
Charcoal my skin
Rip me apart from within
Turn my bones to
Turn my bones to
And my gums line with
They line with
Gunpowder

MONSTER
Monster
With broken wings
Angel
Of fucked up things
You know what I am
You know
What I am
Do not hold me
When judgement calls
Just accept
That I might fall
From a god's grace
I will not try
To save face
Monster with broken wings
Angel
Of somber things
Hold me right
Hold me tight
Higher
Higher
Don't let me fall
Tonight
Tonight
You know what
I might become
Monster
Of fucked up things
Angel
With broken wings
What am I?

What am I?
But an ashen thing
Fallen fledgling
Don't let me
Don't let me
Linger
Black eyes
Meet my demise

RIVER STYX
Row me across River Styx
Row me
Row me

Across river styx
Let me meet the goddess Nyx
Ferryman
Charon
Ferryman
Charon
Will the water foam
And churn
Will I crash and burn
Tip over the side
Fall into endless souls
Trapped in their demise
Ferryman
Charon
Ferryman
Charon
Will the water
Be as black as night
As Nyx herself
When I fall in
When I fall in
To a rising current

VESTIGE
I feel as if
I am not, but
A vestige of myself
Cradled in bloodied hands
I see that in my reflection
Born to
What
Born for
Why
I do not know
I wonder aloud
Smoke puffs from my mouth
The vestige smears
It shrivels up
Exposed
I wonder why

BLANK FACES
Blank faces encircle me
They tell me they are my family
And they ask me what my daddy did
I tell them
I knew my daddy didn't love me
When he duct taped my doggy
And left her in the basement to rot
I said to them
My doggy laid out in piss soaked blankets
Yet he still called all of us thankless
For his efforts
Well he strangled my mother
And called me a retard
Before dragging me down the stairs
By my hair
He called my mother a dumb bitch
And I heard her cries in the air
Well the blank faces didn't care
And so I said
He hates me
I know it
He suffocated me
With blankets and pillows
I would beg to be let go
And scream
Then the blank faces dispersed
They didn't give a damn
And let my sisters continue to get hurt
Cause my mami isn't strong enough
To leave on her own
And so I say

And so I say
My daddy didn't love me
When he duct taped my doggy
And dragged me down the stairs
By my hair
My daddy doesn't love me
Doesn't love my mami
Or my sisters
The blank faces are gone now
Because they don't care

BEAUTIFUL BOY
Beautiful boy
Are you stuck in your skin
In your room
In your bed
In your head
Are you angry at the world
Do you seethe at the softness of your hands
Does running your fingers through your hair make you howl
Do you feel that ache in your jaw
From clenching too hard
Is your neck stiff

IN DARKNESS
I cling to the dark
The way I cling
To your shirt sleeve
The way I
The way I
Cling to the stars
In your eyes
In vibrant purple skies
Starve me
Starve me
Of your anomaly
And
I'll cling
To the dark
The way I cling
To your shirt sleeve

FESTER
My skin festers
Under this fabric
Within these bindings
It peels and blisters
It blisters
Heal me
Heal me
My blood burns
Beneath me
Let it burn
Let it fester
I fester
Under this fabric
Under this

AM I SCARED OF LIVING

Ethanol on my tongue
Ignite me
Am I meant for this
Am I scared of living
Gasoline on my breath
Light a match
Against my finger tips
Strike me
Strike me
Am I scared of living
Ash under my nails
My skin pales
In comparison
Am I meant for this

SHRIKE
You are the shrike
To my branch
Pierce against my thorns
Free me
Feed me
Blood drips down
My tree
Shrike to my beautiful
Free me

HUMMINGBIRD TO A ROSE
Am I so broken
Am I so tired
Am I done yet

Am I done yet
Like a hummingbird to a rose
Life beats through the pain
Will life beat me
And cause me pain
Am I so tired of living
Am I so tired of living
That a hummingbird to a rose
Means nothing
But stardust to the wind
Grind my bones
Grind them to dust
Let the wind take me
Am I done yet
Am I too tired yet
As the wind carries me further
Further
Sway to me
Say to me
That I'm the rose
To your hummingbird

HANG ME IDLE
Hang me idle
Hand me a bit and bridle
And I'll ride out
Stride out
Pried away
Don't let me stay
Don't let me stray
Hang me idle
Hang me by my ankles
And I'll hand you
I'll hand you
A yellow dandelion

STRANGLED
Strangle me
Wrangle me down
Tie me with tape

Bind me down to the ground
Strangle me

CARPENTER BEE
Sting me
Carpenter bee
Make me feel something
Let the blood beed
On my palm
Land on me
Brand me
String me along
Hand me a knife
I will tell you my strife
As I slice open my palm
Sting me
Carpenter bee
Like you know what it feels like
To bleed

PAIN RELIEVER
Pop some acetaminophen
I hope it doesn't kill me
As I reach through

And grab at you
Death with hidden fingers
Come at me
And I'll pop some acetaminophen
Down the bottle
Overdose on pain relievers
Overdose on
Kill me with effexor
Bring me to the brink
Down some medication
Elixir
Pop some acetaminophen

BUILD A SANDCASTLE
Build a sandcastle with me
Let it wash away
With the sea
Sculpt something with me
Don't let it be swept away
With the rest of the debris
Don't hold me
The way you would not hold
Onto a sand castle
Let me wash away in the sea
Let me wash away in the sea

HOLD ME
Hold me as if i am a breath
From passing
Hold me as if I have thorns

Gentle
Priceless
Hold me
Hold me
As if I were already a ghost

RIVER
Drown me in the river
Shackle me
To my own bones

Don't let me up
Don't let me up
I'm down
Down
Drown me in the river
Don't hold me through it
Just let me go
Let me go

SCRAWL YOUR LOVE
Scrawl across my skin
Your name
Yourself

Tattoo your hand print
Above my heart
Against my chest
Tattoo your lips
Across my neck
Scrawl your love
Across my skin

ROT
Flay me
From my body
From this mortal vessel

Don't let me rot
Don't let me rot
In this doomed world
This doomed body
I don't want to rot
I don't want to rot

MANGLED CAT
I am a mangled cat
Hanging on by a thread
Fur split

Blood splattering
Hang onto me
Don't let me hit the concrete
Here the screech of tires
Don't let me smear under the rubber
Mangled cat
Mangled cat
Don't let me fall under

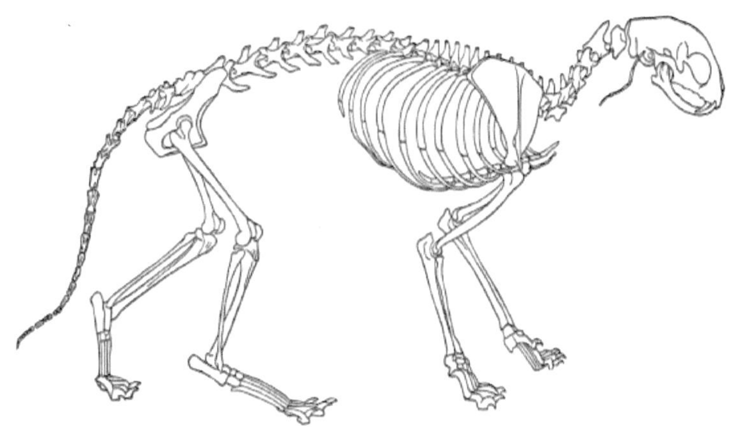